Washington DC
TRAVEL GUIDE 2023

The Ultimate Guide to What to See, Do, and Experience in Washington DC for First-Time Visitors

Eric J. Richardson

Table of Contents

Introduction

Welcome to Washington DC, one of the most iconic cities in the world. As a first-time traveler, you are in for a treat! Washington DC is the capital city of the United States, and it is rich in history, culture, and entertainment. As the home of the federal government, it is a hub of political activity and attracts visitors from around the world who want to experience its iconic landmarks, museums, and monuments.

One of the first things you will notice about Washington DC is its grand architecture and wide streets. The city was designed by French architect Pierre L'Enfant in the late 1700s and features wide avenues and grand public spaces that give it a spacious and majestic feel. The National Mall, for example, is a long, tree-lined park that stretches from the Capitol Building to the Lincoln Memorial and is home to many of the city's iconic landmarks.

In terms of things to do and see, Washington DC has a lot to offer. Its most famous landmarks include the White House, the Lincoln Memorial, the Washington Monument, and the U.S. Capitol Building. The city is also home to dozens of world-class museums, including the Smithsonian Institution, which is the world's largest museum complex and features a wide range of exhibits and collections, from natural history to art and culture.

Beyond its landmarks and museums, Washington DC is also a vibrant city with a thriving food and drink scene, lively music and arts communities, and many outdoor activities to enjoy. You can explore historic neighborhoods, take a bike ride along the Potomac River, attend a festival or concert, or simply relax in one of the city's many parks and green spaces.

Overall, Washington DC is a city that offers something for everyone, whether you are interested in history, politics, culture, or entertainment. As a first-time traveler, be sure to plan ahead and give yourself plenty of time to explore all that this amazing city has to offer. Whether you are here for a few days or a few weeks, you are sure to have an unforgettable experience in Washington DC!

About Washington DC

Washington DC is a city with a rich history and culture that spans more than two centuries. As the capital of the United States, it has played a significant role in shaping the country's political, economic, and cultural landscape.

The history of Washington DC dates back to 1790 when it was established as the capital of the newly formed United States. The city was named after George Washington, the first president of the United States, and was designed by French architect Pierre L'Enfant. L'Enfant's vision for the city was a grand and spacious one, with wide avenues and grand public spaces that created an open and inviting atmosphere.

Throughout its history, Washington DC has been the site of many significant events and milestones. It was the site of the Civil War and played a central role in the Civil Rights Movement. The city has also been the site of many presidential inaugurations, state funerals, and other important ceremonies.

Washington DC is also a city with a rich cultural heritage. The city is home to many world-class museums, including the Smithsonian Institution, which is the largest museum complex in the world. Here, visitors can explore collections that cover everything from natural history to art and culture.

In addition to its museums, Washington DC is a city with a vibrant arts and culture scene. The city is home to many theaters, music venues, and art galleries that showcase the talents of local and international artists. The Kennedy Center for the Performing Arts is a premier venue for music, dance, and theater performances, while the National Gallery of Art houses an impressive collection of art from around the world.

Washington DC is also known for its diverse food scene, which reflects the city's multicultural population. Visitors can enjoy everything from classic American cuisine to international flavors, including Ethiopian, Korean, and Mexican food.

Overall, Washington DC is a city with a rich and complex history and culture. As a first-time traveler, taking the time to explore the city's landmarks, museums, and cultural institutions will give you a deeper understanding and appreciation of this amazing city.

Geography and climate of Washington DC

Washington DC is situated in the mid-Atlantic area of the United States, on the east coast. The city is located on the banks of the Potomac River and encompasses an area of roughly 68 square miles.

The terrain of Washington DC is characterized by low hills and valleys, with an average height of 39 feet above sea level. The city is split into four quadrants by two diagonal avenues, North

Capitol Street and South Capitol Street, which cross the U.S. Capitol Building.

Washington DC has a humid subtropical climate, which is typified by hot, humid summers and cold winters. The city enjoys four different seasons, with temperatures varying from an average high of 89°F (32°C) in July to an average low of 27°F (-3°C) in January.

During the summer months, temperatures may regularly reach into the 90s (Fahrenheit), with high humidity levels making it seem much hotter. Thunderstorms are prevalent throughout the summer, with rare severe storms that may bring heavy rain, high gusts, and hail.

Autumn in Washington DC is moderate and pleasant, with temperatures ranging from the mid-50s to the mid-70s. This is a great season for travelers to explore the city since the weather is warm and there are numerous outdoor festivals and activities going on.

Winter in Washington DC may be chilly and snowy, with temperatures regularly plunging below freezing. Snow is relatively rare throughout the winter months, with an average of around 15 inches of snowfall every year. Visitors should be prepared for chilly weather and wear layers since temperatures might change throughout the day.

Spring in Washington DC is moderate and pleasant, with temperatures ranging from the mid-50s to the mid-70s. This is a popular period for tourists to explore the city's parks and gardens, as the cherry blossoms begin to bloom in late March and early April.

Tourists should be prepared for a range of weather conditions depending on the time of year they come, and dress appropriately to make the most of their vacation.

Why visit Washington DC?

There are innumerable reasons to visit Washington DC as a first-time visitor. From historical sites and iconic monuments to world-class museums and cultural events, the city provides something for everyone. These are some of the best reasons to visit Washington DC:

History: Being the capital of the United States, Washington DC is rich in history. Tourists may visit the National Mall, where they can view the Lincoln Memorial, the Washington Monument, and the Vietnam Veterans Memorial, among other notable sites. The city is also home to various museums and historic places, including the Smithsonian Institution, which holds some of the world's most significant relics and exhibitions.

Politics: Washington DC is the seat of the U.S. government, and tourists may view the U.S. Capitol Building, the White House, and the Supreme Court, among other major government structures. Visitors may also observe democracy in action by attending a session of Congress or a Supreme Court hearing.

Culture: Washington DC is a bustling city with a varied population, and tourists may experience its various cultural attractions, including live music, theater, and dance events, as well as culinary festivals and street fairs.

Education: Washington DC is home to several of the country's premier institutions, including Georgetown University and George Washington University. Visitors may take use of the city's intellectual resources by attending a lecture or seminar, or by visiting one of the numerous research institutes situated in the vicinity.

Natural beauty: Although being a busy metropolis, Washington DC is also home to various parks and green areas, including Rock Creek Park, the National Arboretum, and the Tidal Basin, where tourists may view the famed cherry blossoms in the spring.

Whether you're interested in politics, education, or just soaking in the city's colorful vibe, Washington DC has something to offer everyone.

Overview of the City and Its Neighborhoods

Washington DC is a vibrant city with many distinct neighborhoods, each with its character and charm. Here is an overview of the city's neighborhoods and what they have to offer:

Downtown: Located in the heart of the city, Downtown Washington DC is home to many of the city's most famous landmarks, including the National Mall, the White House, and the Smithsonian museums. This area is bustling with activity during the day, with many government buildings and businesses located here. At night, it is quieter but still has a vibrant nightlife scene with many restaurants, bars, and theaters.

Georgetown: Located in the northwest part of the city, Georgetown is one of the city's oldest neighborhoods and is known for its historic row houses, boutique shops, and cobblestone streets. It is also home to Georgetown University and the historic C&O Canal, which offers a beautiful place to take a walk or go for a bike ride.

Dupont Circle: Located in the northwest part of the city, Dupont Circle is a diverse and cosmopolitan neighborhood that is home to many embassies, cultural institutions, and restaurants. It is also known for its beautiful parks and historic architecture.

Adams Morgan: Located in the northwest part of the city, Adams Morgan is a diverse neighborhood that is known for its eclectic mix of bars, restaurants, and shops. It is also home to the historic Meridian Hill Park, which offers beautiful views of the city and is a popular spot for picnics and outdoor concerts.

Capitol Hill: Located in the southeast part of the city, Capitol Hill is home to the U.S. Capitol Building, the Supreme Court, and many government buildings. It is also known for its beautiful row houses and historic architecture, as well as its many restaurants and bars.

Shaw: Located in the northwest part of the city, Shaw is a rapidly developing neighborhood that is home to many new restaurants, bars, and shops. It is also home to the historic Howard Theatre and the African American Civil War Museum.

Washington DC is a city of diverse neighborhoods, each with its unique personality and attractions. Whether you're interested in history, and culture, or simply exploring new areas, there is something to discover in every part of the city.

Chapter1: Getting to and around Washington DC

Transportation options to Washington DC

Washington, D.C., being the capital of the United States, is a popular tourist destination for both domestic and international visitors. There are many modes of transportation accessible to get to Washington, D.C., including airlines, trains, buses, and vehicles.

1. Flights: Ronald Reagan Washington National Airport (DCA), Dulles International Airport (IAD), and Baltimore/Washington International Thurgood Marshall Airport (BWI) serve the Washington, D.C. area (BWI). DCA, situated only a few miles south in Virginia,

is the closest to the city core. IAD is about 26 miles west of D.C. in Virginia, while BWI is approximately 30 miles northeast of D.C. in Maryland. The three airports provide a wide range of local and international flights, with several major airlines servicing the region.

2. Trains: Amtrak runs many rail lines to and from Washington D.C., including the Northeast Regional, Acela Express, and Capitol Limited. Union Station is the major railway station in Washington D.C., situated in the middle of the city. Train travel may be a pleasant and convenient choice, particularly for individuals going from neighboring cities such as New York or Philadelphia.

3. Buses: Several bus companies operate routes to and from Washington D.C.,

including Greyhound, Megabus, and BoltBus. These buses offer an affordable option for travel and often have several pickup and drop-off locations throughout the city.

4. Driving: Driving to Washington D.C. can be a convenient option for those who live nearby or who are planning a road trip. Major highways such as Interstate 95 and Interstate 66 provide easy access to the city. However, traffic can be heavy during peak hours, and parking in the city can be difficult and expensive.

Once you arrive in Washington D.C., there are several transportation options available to get around the city. The Metrorail system, also known as the Metro, is a subway system that serves the city and surrounding areas. The Metrobus system provides bus service throughout the city and suburbs. Taxis, ride-sharing services such as Uber and Lyft, and bike-sharing programs such as Capital Bikeshare are also available.

When planning your trip to Washington D.C., consider the transportation options available and choose the one that best fits your budget and travel needs. With its many transportation options, getting to and around Washington D.C. is easy and convenient.

Entry requirements and Travel Insurance

It's important to make sure you meet the entry requirements and have appropriate travel insurance coverage when planning a trip to Washington D.C. By taking the time to review the entry requirements and purchasing a comprehensive travel insurance policy, you can help ensure a safe and enjoyable trip to this historic city. Here's what you need to know:

Entry Requirements: If you're a citizen of one of the Visa Waiver Program countries, you can enter the U.S. without a visa for up to 90 days as long as you have a valid Electronic System for Travel Authorization (ESTA). You can apply for an ESTA online at the U.S. Customs and Border Protection website. If you're not a citizen of a Visa Waiver Program country, you will need to apply for a visa at a U.S. Embassy or Consulate. Make sure to check the entry requirements well in advance of your travel date.

Travel Insurance: While travel insurance is not mandatory for entry into the U.S., it is highly recommended. Travel insurance can help protect you in case of unforeseen events such as flight cancellations, medical emergencies, or lost or stolen luggage. Make sure to carefully review the policy to ensure it covers any specific needs you may have, such as adventure activities or pre-existing medical conditions.

When purchasing travel insurance, be sure to consider the following:

- Coverage: Make sure your policy covers the activities you plan to do and any pre-existing medical conditions you have.
- Duration: Ensure your policy covers the entire length of your trip.
- Emergency medical coverage: Make sure you have adequate coverage for medical emergencies, including emergency medical transportation.
- Cancellation and trip interruption coverage: This can help protect you if you need to cancel or cut short your trip due to unforeseen events.

- Lost or stolen baggage coverage: This can help cover the cost of replacing lost or stolen items.

It's important to purchase travel insurance as soon as you book your trip to ensure maximum coverage.

Packing list

Here's a comprehensive packing list for first-time travelers to Washington DC:

1. Comfortable walking shoes: You will likely be doing a lot of walking in Washington DC, so it's important to pack comfortable shoes that can handle lots of walking.

2. Lightweight clothing: Washington DC can get hot and humid in the summer, so pack lightweight clothing that breathes well. However, it can also get chilly in the evenings and during the winter months, so

pack layers that you can easily add or remove as needed.

3. Rain gear: Washington DC can experience occasional showers, so it's a good idea to pack a waterproof jacket or umbrella.

4. Sunscreen and sunglasses: The sun can be strong in Washington DC, so it's important to protect your skin and eyes with sunscreen and sunglasses.

5. Hat: A hat can also help protect your skin and keep you cool in the sun.

6. Camera: There are many photo-worthy sights in Washington DC, so don't forget your camera or smartphone to capture your memories.

7. Backpack or tote bag: A backpack or tote bag can be useful for carrying water, snacks, and other essentials while exploring the city.

8. **Power bank and charging cables:** To keep your electronic devices charged while on the go, pack a power bank and charging cables.

9. **ID and travel documents:** Be sure to bring a valid form of ID, such as a passport or driver's license, and any necessary travel documents, such as your airline tickets or hotel reservation confirmations.

10. **Medications:** If you take prescription medications, be sure to pack enough for your entire trip, along with any necessary medical supplies.

11. **Travel-sized toiletries:** To save space in your luggage, pack travel-sized toiletries, such as shampoo, conditioner, and toothpaste.

12. **Cash and credit cards:** While many places in Washington DC accept credit cards, it's

always a good idea to have some cash on hand for small purchases or tipping.

By packing these essential items, you'll be well-prepared for your trip to Washington DC, and able to enjoy all the city has to offer.

Public transportation in Washington DC

Washington DC is a city with an extensive public transportation system, which makes getting around the city relatively easy and affordable. Here is a comprehensive guide to public transportation in Washington DC for first-time travelers:

1. Metro: The Washington Metro is a subway system that serves the whole city and its environs. It is the most efficient mode of transportation in the city, and it is especially beneficial for travelling to and

from the National Mall and other tourist destinations. During weekdays, the Metro runs from 5:00 a.m. to midnight, and on weekends, it runs from 7:00 a.m. to midnight. Prices are calculated depending on distance and vary from $2.00 to $6.00 for a single journey. For $10.00, visitors may get a SmarTrip card, which is a reusable plastic card that can be filled with money for fares. Metro stations and most convenience shops sell SmarTrip cards.

2. Bus: The Washington DC bus system is run by the Washington Metropolitan Area Transit Authority (WMATA). It is an affordable and efficient way to get around the city, particularly if you're traveling to neighborhoods that are not serviced by the Metro. Fares are $2.00 for a single ride, and visitors can also use a SmarTrip card

to pay for their fares. There are several different bus routes in the city, and it's important to check the WMATA website or use the Transit app to plan your route.

3. Circulator: The DC Circulator is a bus system that serves specific areas of the city, including downtown, Georgetown, and Capitol Hill. Fares are $1.00 per ride, and visitors can also use a SmarTrip card to pay for their fares. The Circulator is a great option for getting around the city quickly and efficiently, particularly if you're only traveling short distances.

4. Taxis and Ride-Sharing Services: Taxis are readily available in Washington DC, and visitors can easily hail a cab on the street or use a ride-sharing app like Uber or Lyft. Taxis and ride-sharing services are more expensive than public transportation, but they can be a convenient option if you're

traveling with a group or need to get somewhere quickly.

5. Bike Sharing: Washington DC also has a bike-sharing system called Capital Bikeshare, which allows visitors to rent bikes by the hour or day. There are stations located throughout the city, and riders can use the bikes to explore the city's many bike trails and paths.

Washington DC has a robust and affordable public transportation system that makes getting around the city relatively easy and stress-free. By using the Metro, bus, Circulator, or other transportation options, you can explore the city's many attractions and neighborhoods without breaking the bank.

Taxis and ridesharing in Washington DC

Taxis and ridesharing services are popular and convenient ways to get around Washington D.C. for tourists and locals alike. Here is what you need to know about taxis and ridesharing in Washington D.C.

Taxis: Taxis in Washington D.C. are regulated by the D.C. Taxicab Commission, and fares are metered. There are several taxi companies in the city, including Yellow Cab and Uber Taxi. Taxis can be hailed on the street or found at designated taxi stands throughout the city. It is important to note that taxi fares can be higher during peak hours and may include additional charges for luggage, tolls, and credit card processing fees.

Ridesharing: Ridesharing services such as Uber and Lyft are widely available in Washington D.C.

These services allow passengers to request a ride using a smartphone app and pay through the app using a credit card. Ridesharing fares are typically lower than taxi fares, and riders can choose from several different options, including standard rides, shared rides, and luxury rides.

Safety: When using taxis or ridesharing services in Washington D.C., it is important to prioritize safety. Always check the license plate and driver information before getting into a car, and ensure that the driver matches the photo on the app. Be cautious of fake or unlicensed drivers, especially if they approach you on the street. If you feel unsafe at any point during the ride, you can call 911 or the police.

Accessibility: Both taxis and ridesharing services offer accessible options for passengers with disabilities. In Washington D.C., all taxis are required to be wheelchair accessible, and ridesharing services offer options for passengers with disabilities as well. When requesting a ride, be sure to select the accessible option and provide any necessary information about your needs.

Car rentals in Washington DC

If you prefer to have your vehicle while exploring Washington DC, renting a car is a great option. Here is a comprehensive guide to car rentals in Washington DC for first-time travelers:

Rental Companies: There are several rental car companies located in and around Washington DC, including major chains like Hertz, Enterprise, and Avis. You can easily find and book a rental car online or at the rental car counters located at the airport or other transportation hubs in the city.

Cost: The cost of renting a car in Washington DC varies depending on several factors, such as the type of car you choose, the rental company, and the duration of your rental. On average, the cost of a rental car in Washington DC can range from $30 to $100 per day, depending on these factors.

Requirements: To rent a car in Washington DC, you must have a valid driver's license, be at least 21 years old, and have a major credit card in your name. Some rental car companies may have additional requirements, such as a minimum age requirement of 25 or additional insurance coverage.

Insurance: It's important to note that rental car companies typically offer insurance coverage for an additional fee. This coverage may include collision damage waiver, personal accident insurance, and liability insurance. It's important to carefully review the rental car agreement and insurance options before renting a car to ensure you have the coverage you need.

Parking: Parking in Washington DC can be challenging and expensive, particularly in the downtown area. Some rental car companies offer parking options, but you may need to pay an additional fee. It's important to research parking options in the area you plan to visit and budget accordingly.

Navigation: Navigating Washington DC can be challenging, particularly during rush hour or in areas with heavy traffic. Many rental car companies offer GPS navigation systems for an additional fee, which can help get around the city. Overall, renting a car in Washington DC can be a convenient option for exploring the city and surrounding areas. However, it's important to carefully consider the cost, requirements, insurance coverage, and parking options before making a decision. By doing your research and planning ahead, you can enjoy a stress-free and affordable rental car experience in Washington DC.

Chapter2: Accommodations in Washington DC

Types of accommodations in Washington DC

Washington DC offers a variety of accommodations to suit every budget and preference, ranging from luxurious hotels to budget-friendly hostels. Here are the different types of accommodations available in Washington DC and their average costs:

1. Hotels: Washington DC has numerous hotels catering to all budgets, from luxury to budget-friendly. The cost of hotels can vary depending on the location, amenities, and season. On average, a mid-range hotel in Washington DC can cost between $150 to $300 per night, while a luxury hotel can cost upwards of $500 per night.

2. **Bed and Breakfasts (B&Bs): B&Bs are a popular option for those looking for a more intimate and cozy experience. B&Bs in Washington DC are typically smaller and have fewer amenities than hotels, but they offer a more personalized touch. The average cost of a B&B in Washington DC ranges from $100 to $200 per night.**

3. **Vacation Rentals: Vacation rentals, such as apartments, condos, and houses, are a great option for those looking for a home away from home experience. They offer more space and privacy than a hotel or B&B, and they are a good option for families or large groups. The average cost of a vacation rental in Washington DC varies depending on the size and location but can range from $150 to $500 per night.**

4. **Hostels: Hostels are a budget-friendly option for solo travelers or those traveling**

with a group. They offer shared rooms or private rooms at an affordable cost. Hostels in Washington DC typically cost between $20 to $60 per night, depending on the amenities and location.

5. Camping: For those who enjoy the great outdoors, camping is a great option. Washington DC has several campgrounds in nearby areas that offer tent and RV camping. The cost of camping ranges from $20 to $50 per night, depending on the campground and amenities.

When choosing your accommodation in Washington DC, consider your budget, location preferences, and the amenities you require. Booking in advance can also help you save money and ensure availability during the peak travel season.

Best areas to stay in Washington DC

Washington, D.C. is a bustling and varied city with a wide range of areas to discover. These are some of the greatest places to stay for first-time visitors:

1. Downtown: This is the heart of the city and the best place to stay if you want to be close to all the major attractions. From the White House to the National Mall, everything is within walking distance. The area is also home to a variety of hotels, restaurants, and shops.

2. Dupont Circle: This neighborhood is known for its trendy restaurants, art galleries, and nightlife. It's a great place to stay if you're looking for a lively atmosphere and want to be close to the city's cultural scene.

3. **Georgetown: This historic neighborhood is home to some of the city's most charming streets and architecture. It's also a great place to shop, with many boutiques and specialty stores. While it's a bit further from the major tourist attractions, it's still within walking distance or a short metro ride away.**

4. **Capitol Hill: Capitol Hill is home to the United States Capitol and numerous other federal buildings. It's a calmer neighborhood than downtown, but it's still close to many of the city's big attractions. It's also a terrific spot to stay if you want to see the city from a different perspective.**

5. **Adams Morgan: This neighborhood is known for its diverse food scene, lively nightlife, and colorful street art. It's a bit further from the major tourist attractions, but it's a great place to stay if you're**

looking for a unique and authentic experience of the city.

When choosing a neighborhood to stay in, it's important to consider your budget, the type of experience you're looking for, and your proximity to the attractions you want to visit. Many neighborhoods are well-connected by the city's metro system, making it easy to get around. By choosing the right neighborhood, you can make the most of your trip to Washington D.C., and experience all the city has to offer.

Recommended hotels in Washington DC

Washington DC offers a wide range of hotels, each with its unique style, amenities, and location. Here are some recommended hotels in Washington DC, along with their average costs per night:

1. **The Hay-Adams:** The Hay-Adams is a luxurious hotel located across from the White House. The hotel offers elegant rooms and suites with views of the city, as well as an on-site restaurant and fitness center. Average cost per night: $500-$800.

2. **The Watergate Hotel:** The Watergate Hotel is an iconic hotel located near the Georgetown neighborhood. The hotel offers stylish rooms and suites with views of the Potomac River, as well as an indoor pool, spa, and rooftop bar. Average cost per night: $300-$600.

3. **Kimpton Hotel Monaco Washington DC:** The Kimpton Hotel Monaco is a boutique hotel located in the heart of the city, near popular attractions such as the National Mall and the Smithsonian museums. The hotel offers stylish rooms and suites with unique decor, as well as an on-site

restaurant and fitness center. Average cost per night: $200-$400.

4. **The Mayflower Hotel, Autograph Collection: The Mayflower Hotel is a historic hotel located in the downtown area, close to popular attractions and restaurants. The hotel offers elegant rooms and suites with modern amenities, as well as an on-site restaurant and fitness center. Average cost per night: $200-$400.**

5. **The LINE Hotel DC: The LINE Hotel DC is a trendy hotel located in the Adams Morgan neighborhood. The hotel offers stylish rooms and suites with unique decor, as well as several on-site dining options and a rooftop bar with city views. Average cost per night: $150-$300.**

6. **Hotel Hive: Hotel Hive is a budget-friendly hotel located in the Foggy Bottom neighborhood, near the George**

Washington University campus. The hotel offers modern and compact rooms with amenities such as free Wi-Fi and a fitness center. Average cost per night: $100-$200.

These are just a few of the many hotels available in Washington DC. When choosing your hotel, consider your budget, location preferences, and the amenities you require. It's also a good idea to book in advance, especially during peak travel season, to ensure availability and get the best rates.

Alternative lodging options in Washington DC

In addition to traditional hotels, there are many alternative lodging options available in Washington D.C. that offer unique experiences and can be more budget-friendly.

Hostels: For budget-conscious tourists, hostels are an excellent alternative. They provide shared dormitory-style accommodations as well as individual rooms at a lesser cost than hotels. HI Washington D.C. and Duo Housing are two prominent Washington D.C. hostels.

Cost: Hostel prices in Washington D.C. start at around $25 per night for a shared dorm room, while private rooms start at around $70 per night.

Vacation Rentals: Vacation rentals, such as Airbnb and VRBO, offer the opportunity to stay in a private apartment or house in the city. This can be a great option for families or groups who want more space and the ability to cook their meals.

Cost: The cost of vacation rentals in Washington D.C. varies depending on the location and amenities. Prices can range from $50 per night for a shared room to over $500 per night for a luxury home.

Bed and Breakfasts: Bed and breakfasts offer a more personalized experience than traditional hotels. They typically include a home-cooked breakfast and offer a cozy atmosphere. Some popular bed and breakfasts in Washington D.C. include the Embassy Circle Guest House and Swann House.

Cost: Bed and breakfast prices in Washington D.C. start at around $100 per night for a basic room, with prices increasing for larger rooms and more amenities.

Co-living Spaces: Co-living spaces are a newer type of lodging that offers a community-focused living experience. They typically offer private bedrooms and shared common areas, such as kitchens and living rooms. Some popular co-living spaces in Washington D.C. include Common and WeLive.

Cost: Co-living spaces in Washington D.C. start at around $1,000 per month for a private room and shared common areas.

When choosing an alternative lodging option, it's important to consider your budget, the location, and the amenities you require. Many of these options offer unique experiences and can be a great way to save money while still enjoying all that Washington D.C. has to offer.

Chapter3: Top Attractions and Activities in Washington DC

Top Attractions

Washington, D.C. is a city with a rich history and many important landmarks and monuments. Here are the top 20 attractions to see in Washington, D.C. for any first-time traveler:

National Mall and Memorial Parks: This vast parkland is home to some of the city's most famous landmarks, including the Lincoln Memorial, the Washington Monument, and the Vietnam Veterans Memorial.

Smithsonian Institution Museums: The Smithsonian Institution runs 19 museums and galleries in the Washington, D.C. region, including the National Air and Space Museum, the National Museum of American History, and The National Museum of Natural History. The

Smithsonian museums are open to the public for free.

The White House and Capitol Hill: The White House is the official residence of the President of the United States, while the Capitol is where Congress meets. Both buildings are available for guided visits to the general public.

Monuments and Memorials: Apart from the memorials on the National Mall, the city is home to several other monuments and memorials, including the Jefferson Memorial, the Franklin Delano Roosevelt Memorial, and the Martin Luther King Jr. Memorial.

Arlington National Cemetery: The ultimate resting place of many American heroes, including President John F. Kennedy and the Challenger space shuttle crew.

National Zoo: The National Zoo is home to more than 2,000 animals of 400 species, including giant pandas, elephants, and lions.

The National Cathedral: This stunning Gothic cathedral is the sixth largest in the world and has been the site of many national events, including presidential funerals.

Library of Congress: The Library of Congress is the world's biggest library, housing millions of books, maps, and manuscripts.

National Gallery of Art: This museum features an extensive collection of European and American art from the Middle Ages to the present day.

Supreme Court: Visitors can attend oral arguments at the Supreme Court and tour the building, which is one of the most important in the country.

United States Holocaust Memorial Museum: A somber and thought-provoking museum dedicated to the memory of the Holocaust and its victims.

National Portrait Gallery: An art museum featuring portraits of prominent American figures throughout history.

National Archives Museum: Home to the original copies of the United States Constitution, Declaration of Independence, and Bill of Rights.

Ford's Theatre: The site of President Abraham Lincoln's assassination, now a historic theater and museum.

International Spy Museum: A unique museum dedicated to the history and techniques of espionage and intelligence gathering.

National Museum of Women in the Arts: A museum showcasing the works of women artists from around the world.

The Phillips Collection: A museum of modern art featuring works by Impressionist, Post-Impressionist, and modern artists.

The Kennedy Center: A performing arts center and venue for music, theater, and dance performances.

National Museum of African American History and Culture: A museum exploring the history and culture of African Americans in the United States.

Georgetown: A historic neighborhood with beautiful architecture, boutique shops, and restaurants.

These attractions are just the tip of the iceberg when it comes to all the amazing things to see and do in Washington, D.C. No matter what your interests are, there is something for everyone in this vibrant and historic city.

Cultural and Entertainment Activities in Washington DC

Washington D.C. is a city with a rich cultural and entertainment scene, offering a wide range of activities for first-time travelers to enjoy. Here are the top 20 cultural and entertainment activities in Washington D.C.:

1. Visit the Smithsonian Museums: The Smithsonian museums are a collection of 19 museums and galleries, including the National Air and Space Museum, the National Museum of American History, and the National Museum of Natural History. Admission is free for all museums.

2. Walk the National Mall: The National Mall is a landscaped park that stretches from the Lincoln Memorial to the U.S. Capitol. It is home to many iconic

landmarks, such as the Washington Monument and the Reflecting Pool.

3. Tour the White House: Visitors can tour the White House by submitting a request through their Member of Congress at least 21 days in advance.

4. Watch a performance at the Kennedy Center: The Kennedy Center is a performing arts center that hosts a variety of shows, from ballet to theater to music.

5. Visit the National Archives: The Declaration of Independence, the Constitution, and the Bill of Rights are among the key historical documents housed in the National Archives.

6. See the monuments at night: Many of Washington D.C.'s monuments are lit up at night, providing a beautiful and unique view of the city.

7. Explore the National Zoo: The National Zoo is a free zoo that is home to over 2,700 animals.

8. Visit the Library of Congress: The Library of Congress is the largest library in the world and houses millions of books, manuscripts, and other materials.

9. See a show at the Ford's Theatre: The Ford's Theatre is the site of President Lincoln's assassination and now hosts a variety of shows and events.

10. Walk through Georgetown: Georgetown is a historic neighborhood with beautiful architecture, boutique shops, and delicious restaurants.

11. Visit the United States Holocaust Memorial Museum: The United States Holocaust Memorial Museum is a powerful museum that tells the story of the

Holocaust through artifacts, exhibits, and personal stories.

12. Take a bike tour: Biking is a great way to see the city and there are many bike tours available.

13. Visit the National Gallery of Art: The National Gallery of Art is home to thousands of works of art, from paintings to sculptures to photographs.

14. Take a tour of the U.S. Capitol: Visitors can tour the U.S. Capitol by submitting a request through their Member of Congress.

15. Visit the National Museum of African American History and Culture: The National Museum of African American History and Culture is a Smithsonian museum that tells the story of African American history and culture.

16. Explore the Tidal Basin: The Tidal Basin is a beautiful waterfront area with views of the Jefferson Memorial and cherry blossom trees in the spring.

17. See a game at Nationals Park: Nationals Park is the home stadium of the Washington Nationals baseball team.

18. Visit the National Museum of the American Indian: The National Museum of the American Indian is a Smithsonian museum that tells the story of Native American history and culture.

19. Take a tour of the Supreme Court: Visitors can tour the Supreme Court by submitting a request through their Member of Congress.

20. Walk through the National Arboretum: The National Arboretum is a 446-acre

botanical garden with beautiful gardens, forests, and trails to explore.

These are just a few of the many cultural and entertainment activities that Washington D.C. has to offer. With so many options, there's something for everyone to enjoy in this vibrant city.

Sports and outdoor activities

Washington, D.C. may be known for its politics and history, but there are also plenty of outdoor and sports activities for visitors to enjoy. Here are the top 20 sports and outdoor activities in Washington, D.C.:

1. Visit the National Mall: The National Mall is a great place to walk, run, or bike, with scenic views of the monuments and the Potomac River.

2. Hiking and Biking: Rock Creek Park has over 32 miles of hiking and biking trails, with options for all skill levels.

3. Kayaking on the Potomac: Rent a kayak or stand-up paddleboard and explore the Potomac River, with views of the monuments and the Kennedy Center.

4. Running: Join one of the many running groups in the city or participate in a race such as the Cherry Blossom 10 Mile Run in the spring.

5. Golfing: Washington, D.C. has several public and private golf courses, including the East Potomac Golf Course which offers stunning views of the National Mall.

6. Tennis: The Rock Creek Park Tennis Center has 25 courts, including hard and clay courts, and hosts the Citi Open tournament each summer.

7. Baseball: Catch a Washington Nationals baseball game at Nationals Park.

8. Soccer: D.C. United plays Major League Soccer at Audi Field, which also hosts other sporting events and concerts.

9. Ultimate Frisbee: Join a pickup game or watch a professional game with the D.C. Breeze team.

10. Roller Skating: Roller skating is a popular activity in the city, with several rinks available including the Anacostia Roller Skating Pavilion.

11. Ice Skating: During the winter months, enjoy outdoor ice skating at the National Gallery of Art Sculpture Garden or Canal Park.

12. Horseback Riding: The Rock Creek Park Horse Center offers trail rides and lessons for all skill levels.

13. Zip Lining: The Go Ape Treetop Adventure Course offers zip lines, rope bridges, and other obstacles for an exhilarating experience.

14. Disc Golf: Try your hand at disc golf at one of the city's several courses, including the Kenilworth Park & Aquatic Gardens course.

15. Skateboarding: The city has several skate parks, including the popular Maloof Skate Park at RFK Stadium.

16. Fishing: The Potomac River offers a variety of fishing opportunities, with several companies offering guided trips and equipment rentals.

17. Pickleball: The sport of pickleball is growing in popularity in the city, with several indoor and outdoor courts available.

18. Yoga: Take a yoga class at one of the city's many studios or join a free outdoor class at the Georgetown Waterfront.

19. Rowing: The Potomac River is a popular spot for rowing, with several rowing clubs and companies offering lessons and rentals.

20. Outdoor Concerts: During the summer months, enjoy free outdoor concerts at Yards Park or attend the annual Jazz in the Garden series at the National Gallery of Art Sculpture Garden.

Washington, D.C. has a wide variety of sports and outdoor activities for visitors to enjoy, from running and hiking to kayaking and fishing. Whether you're a sports enthusiast or just looking for a way to enjoy the great outdoors, there's something for everyone in this vibrant city.

Day Trips and Excursions from Washington DC

As a first-time traveler to Washington DC, it's always great to explore nearby attractions outside the city. Here are some of the best day trips and excursions that you can take from Washington DC:

1. **Alexandria, VA:** Located just 8 miles south of Washington DC, Alexandria is a charming historic town with cobblestone streets and 18th-century architecture. You can visit museums, enjoy great food, and explore the beautiful waterfront.

2. **Annapolis, MD:** Annapolis, the capital of Maryland, is a beautiful and historic city located just an hour away from DC. It is known for its beautiful architecture, maritime history, and the United States Naval Academy. You can take a stroll around the harbor or visit the Maryland

State House, the oldest state capitol still in continuous legislative use.

3. Baltimore, MD: Baltimore, known as "Charm City," is located just an hour away from Washington DC. It is famous for its Inner Harbor, National Aquarium, and Fort McHenry, the birthplace of the Star-Spangled Banner. You can also explore the historic neighborhoods of Fells Point and Canton or visit the world-famous Johns Hopkins Hospital.

4. Gettysburg, PA: Gettysburg is a historic town located approximately 80 miles northwest of Washington DC. It is best known for the Battle of Gettysburg during the American Civil War, and you can visit the Gettysburg National Military Park to learn more about its history. You can also

explore the quaint shops and restaurants in downtown Gettysburg.

5. Shenandoah National Park, VA: Shenandoah National Park is located approximately 75 miles west of Washington DC, and covers over 200,000 acres of scenic beauty. You can explore the park on a hike, drive the Skyline Drive, or visit the historic Big Meadows Lodge. You can also see wildlife such as black bears, white-tailed deer, and wild turkeys.

These are just a few of the many great day trips and excursions that you can take from Washington DC. Depending on your interests, you can also consider visiting other nearby attractions such as Mount Vernon, Harpers Ferry, or the Chesapeake Bay.

Chapter4: Dining and Drinking in Washington DC

Local cuisine and specialties

Washington DC is a melting pot of cultures, and its culinary scene is no exception. As a first-time traveler, you should explore the city's local cuisine and specialties to get a taste of what makes the city unique.

One of the most famous local specialties is the half-smoke, a sausage made of a blend of pork and beef that is smoked and grilled to perfection. You can try it at Ben's Chili Bowl, a popular restaurant in the U Street Corridor.
Maryland Blue Crabs are another must-try dish in the DC area. These crabs are steamed and seasoned with Old Bay seasoning, giving them a

unique flavor. You can enjoy them at seafood restaurants like The Salt Line or The Wharf.

The city also has a large Ethiopian community, and Ethiopian cuisine is one of its signature dishes. It includes injera, a sourdough flatbread, spiced meats and vegetables, and a variety of dipping sauces. You can try it at restaurants like Etete or Dukem.

Mumbo sauce is a sweet and tangy sauce that is a staple in many Washington DC fast-food restaurants. It is commonly served with fried chicken or french fries, and you can find it at local carry-outs or soul food restaurants.

The Eastern Market is a historic indoor market that has been in operation since 1873. It offers a variety of fresh produce, meats, and baked goods from local vendors. You can also find a range of food stalls serving everything from oysters to empanadas.

Washington DC is also famous for its cupcakes. Several popular cupcake shops like Georgetown Cupcake and Baked & Wired offer a variety of flavors, including red velvet, chocolate, and vanilla.

The city has a thriving craft beer scene, with many local breweries offering unique and flavorful brews. Some of the best breweries to visit include Bluejacket, DC Brau, and Atlas Brew Works.

These are just a few of the many local cuisines and specialties that you can enjoy in Washington DC. With so many options to choose from, there is something for every taste bud.

Best restaurants in Washington DC

Washington, D.C. is home to a diverse range of culinary options, from upscale restaurants to casual eateries serving delicious street food. Here are some of the best restaurants to try during your visit to Washington, D.C.

1. **Le Diplomate:** This French bistro is one of the most popular restaurants in D.C., with classic French cuisine and a cozy atmosphere.

2. **Rose's Luxury:** This Capitol Hill eatery is known for its innovative cuisine, including dishes like pork sausage and lychee salad.

3. **Komi:** This upscale Greek restaurant offers a tasting menu featuring a variety of seafood, meat, and vegetarian dishes.

4. **Maydan:** This Middle Eastern restaurant serves wood-fired dishes like lamb shoulder and whole fish.

5. **Fiola:** This Italian restaurant offers classic dishes like spaghetti carbonara and seafood risotto in an elegant setting.

6. Rasika: This Indian restaurant is known for its modern take on traditional dishes, including a unique black cod with honey and dill.

7. Little Serow: This Thai restaurant serves a tasting menu of Northern Thai dishes, including spicy salads and curries.

8. Founding Farmers: This farm-to-table restaurant offers American comfort food like chicken and waffles and mac and cheese.

9. Bad Saint: This Filipino restaurant serves authentic dishes like pork belly adobo and crispy pata.

10. Oyamel: This Mexican restaurant serves small plates like tacos and ceviche in a colorful setting.

11. Zaytinya: This Mediterranean restaurant serves small plates like hummus and lamb kebabs.

12. Iron Gate: This Mediterranean-inspired restaurant serves dishes like octopus and grilled lamb chops in a historic carriage house.

13. Sushi Taro: This Japanese restaurant offers a wide variety of sushi and sashimi dishes, as well as cooked dishes like tempura and grilled meats.

14. Pineapple and Pearls: This Michelin-starred restaurant offers a tasting menu of modern American cuisine.

15. The Dabney: This farm-to-table restaurant serves seasonal dishes like roasted carrots and smoked pork.

16. Plume: This Michelin-starred restaurant serves French cuisine in an elegant setting, with dishes like seared foie gras and lobster risotto.

17. Thip Khao: This Laotian restaurant serves traditional dishes like papaya salad and pork belly in a cozy atmosphere.

18. Unconventional Diner: This casual diner serves creative takes on classic dishes like meatloaf and fried chicken.

19. All Purpose Pizzeria: This pizza joint serves Neapolitan-style pizza with creative toppings like roasted cauliflower and anchovy.

20. Compass Rose: This cozy restaurant serves dishes inspired by street food from around the world, like Georgian khachapuri and Israeli shakshuka.

Washington, D.C. has a wide variety of restaurants to suit every taste and budget, from high-end French bistros to casual eateries serving street food. Be sure to try some of these top restaurants during your visit to the city.

Food trucks and street food in Washington DC

Washington DC's food truck and street food scene is a popular and affordable option for locals and visitors alike. With hundreds of food trucks and street vendors scattered throughout the city, you're sure to find a delicious and unique meal on the go.

One of the most famous food trucks in the city is DC Empanadas, which serves a variety of savory and sweet empanadas. Their menu includes options like Buffalo chicken, pork, and apple, and even a s'mores empanada for dessert.

Another popular food truck is Fojol Bros, which serves Indian and Ethiopian-inspired cuisine. Their menu includes dishes like butter chicken, injera wraps, and samosas. They also have a colorful and lively setup with a brightly painted truck and staff dressed in colorful costumes.

If you're in the mood for a classic American meal, you can try the Holy Cow food truck. They serve gourmet burgers and fries with unique toppings like bacon jam and truffle aioli. They also offer vegetarian and vegan options.

One of the most popular street food destinations in the city is the Union Market, which features dozens of food vendors offering a range of international cuisine. You can find everything from Korean BBQ to New Orleans-style beignets. In addition to food trucks and street vendors, there are several food festivals and events held throughout the year in DC. The Truckeroo festival, held on select Fridays during the summer months, features dozens of food trucks and live music. The Taste of DC festival, held annually in October, allows visitors to sample dishes from some of the city's top restaurants and food vendors.

When it comes to food trucks and street food in DC, the options are endless. You can find everything from tacos and pizza to Korean BBQ and falafel. The best way to explore this scene is to simply walk around and see what catches your eye.

Craft beer and cocktails in Washington DC

Washington, D.C. has a thriving craft beer and cocktail scene, with many bars and breweries offering unique and innovative drinks. Here are some of the best places to try craft beer and cocktails in the city:

Craft Beer:

1. Bluejacket: This brewery in the Navy Yard neighborhood offers a wide variety of craft beers, including IPAs, stouts, and lagers.

2. The Sovereign: This Belgian-style beer bar in Georgetown has an extensive selection of Belgian and Belgian-style beers, as well as a rotating selection of craft beers from around the world.

3. ChurchKey: This popular bar in Logan Circle has over 50 beers on tap, with a focus on craft beers from local breweries.

4. Right Proper Brewing Company: This Shaw-based brewery serves a variety of craft beers, including IPAs, saisons, and stouts, as well as a rotating selection of seasonal beers.

5. ANXO Cidery & Pintxos Bar: This bar in Truxton Circle specializes in cider, with a

wide selection of cider on tap, as well as Spanish-style pintxos.

Cocktails:

1. **The Columbia Room: This upscale cocktail bar in Shaw offers a variety of innovative cocktails, including seasonal and themed menus.**
2. **Copycat Co.: This speakeasy-style bar in H Street NE offers creative cocktails with a focus on Asian ingredients.**
3. **Barmini by José Andrés: This cocktail bar in Penn Quarter offers unique and inventive cocktails, as well as a tasting menu of small bites.**
4. **Hank's Cocktail Bar: This Dupont Circle bar offers classic cocktails with a twist, as well as a rotating selection of seasonal cocktails.**

5. The Gibson: This speakeasy-style bar in U Street Corridor offers classic cocktails and seasonal specials, as well as a small food menu.

In addition to these bars and breweries, many restaurants in Washington, D.C. also offer craft beer and cocktails. Be sure to ask your server or bartender for recommendations, as there are many hidden gems throughout the city.

Chapter5: Shopping in Washington DC

Washington DC is a city that offers a wide range of shopping opportunities to visitors. From high-end luxury stores to unique boutiques, there is something for every type of shopper. The city's diverse neighborhoods each offer their own unique shopping experience, from trendy Georgetown to eclectic Adams Morgan.

One of the most popular shopping destinations in DC is the Georgetown neighborhood, which is home to a mix of high-end luxury stores and unique boutiques. You can find designer clothing and accessories at stores like Tory Burch and Ralph Lauren, or browse handmade jewelry and unique gifts at boutiques like Proper Topper and the Tiny Jewel Box.

Another popular shopping destination is the Dupont Circle neighborhood, which offers a mix of trendy clothing stores, art galleries, and specialty shops. The neighborhood is home to stores like Current Boutique, which offers high-end consignment clothing, and Kramerbooks & Afterwords Cafe, a popular independent bookstore.

If you're looking for more unique and one-of-a-kind shopping experiences, you can visit the Eastern Market, which is a historic indoor/outdoor market in the Capitol Hill neighborhood. The market features dozens of local vendors selling everything from fresh produce to handmade crafts.

For those who are interested in exploring local and independent businesses, the U Street corridor and Adams Morgan neighborhoods are both known for their eclectic mix of shops and boutiques. You can find vintage clothing and accessories at stores like Meeps, or browse handmade pottery and jewelry at local shops like Little Shop of Clay.

Finally, no trip to DC would be complete without a visit to the Smithsonian Museum stores, which offer a wide range of unique and educational souvenirs. You can find everything from science kits and puzzles to Smithsonian-inspired clothing and accessories.

Overall, shopping in DC is a diverse and exciting experience. Whether you're looking for high-end luxury stores or unique boutiques, you're sure to find something that fits your style and interests in this vibrant city.

Best shopping districts in Washington DC

Washington, D.C. has a variety of shopping districts that cater to different interests and styles. Here are some of the best shopping districts in the city:

Georgetown: This historic neighborhood is known for its charming cobblestone streets and high-end shopping. You'll find a mix of luxury boutiques, designer stores, and popular chains like J.Crew and Anthropologie. Some of the must-visit stores include Tuckernuck, All Saints, and Billy Reid.

Union Market: This indoor market in the NoMa neighborhood is a foodie's paradise, but it also offers unique shopping options. You'll find everything from vintage clothing and handmade jewelry to artisanal home goods and specialty foods. Some of the standout shops include Salt & Sundry, Peregrine Espresso, and the Salt Line Market.

CityCenterDC: This luxury shopping destination in downtown D.C. offers a mix of high-end designer stores, such as Gucci, Louis Vuitton, and Dior, along with more affordable options like Zara and H&M. It's also home to a variety of restaurants and cafes, making it a great spot for a day of shopping and dining.

Dupont Circle: This vibrant neighborhood is home to a variety of independent boutiques, antique stores, and art galleries. You'll find everything from vintage clothing and accessories to unique home decor and gifts. Some of the must-visit shops include Secondi, Miss Pixie's, and Kramerbooks & Afterwords.

Eastern Market: This historic market in Capitol Hill is a great spot to find handmade and artisanal goods, including jewelry, pottery, and paintings. On weekends, the outdoor flea market offers even more shopping options, including vintage clothing and accessories.

Downtown Holiday Market: This outdoor market in downtown D.C. runs during the holiday season and offers a variety of handmade and artisanal goods, including jewelry, home decor, and food items. It's a great place to find unique gifts for loved ones or pick up a souvenir to remember your trip to D.C.

No matter what your shopping interests are, Washington, D.C. has a variety of districts and neighborhoods to explore. Be sure to wear comfortable shoes and bring a tote bag for any purchases you make!

Souvenirs and gifts to buy in Washington DC

Washington, D.C. is a city filled with history, culture, and politics, and it's no surprise that there are many unique and meaningful souvenirs and gifts that you can bring back home with you. Here are some of the best souvenirs and gifts to buy in Washington, D.C.:

1. National Mall Memorabilia: The National Mall is the heart of the city and home to many of the city's most famous landmarks and monuments. There are plenty of gift shops in the area where you can find National Mall memorabilia, including t-shirts, magnets, postcards, and keychains featuring images of the Lincoln Memorial, Washington Monument, and more.

2. Political Memorabilia: As the capital of the United States, Washington, D.C. is home to many government buildings and political institutions. You can find a variety of political memorabilia, including buttons,

bumper stickers, and mugs featuring slogans or images related to U.S. politics.

3. Smithsonian Museum Merchandise: The Smithsonian Institution is the largest museum complex in the world and is made up of 19 museums and galleries. Each museum has its gift shop where you can find unique souvenirs and gifts related to its collection, such as dinosaur toys at the National Museum of Natural History or space-themed gifts at the National Air and Space Museum.

4. Cherry Blossom Merchandise: Each year, Washington, D.C. celebrates the National Cherry Blossom Festival, a springtime celebration of the gift of 3,000 cherry trees given to the city by Japan in 1912. You can find a variety of cherry blossom-themed

souvenirs and gifts, including t-shirts, mugs, and postcards.

5. Handcrafted Goods: There are many local artisans and craftspeople in Washington, D.C. who create unique and beautiful handmade goods. You can find handcrafted jewelry, pottery, textiles, and more at local markets and boutiques throughout the city.

6. Books: Washington, D.C. is a city filled with history and politics, and there are many books available that delve deeper into the city's past and present. You can find books on a variety of topics, including U.S. history, politics, and culture, as well as guidebooks and travel memoirs.

7. Local Foods: Washington, D.C. has a diverse and vibrant food scene, and many local foods and treats make great gifts. Some popular options include Ben's Chili

Bowl's famous half-smokes, Old Bay seasoning, and locally roasted coffee beans. No matter what your interests are, there are plenty of souvenirs and gifts to choose from in Washington, D.C. Be sure to explore the city's many neighborhoods and markets to find unique and meaningful gifts to bring back home with you.

Markets and boutiques in Washington DC

Washington DC is home to a variety of markets and boutiques that offer a unique shopping experience to visitors. From artisanal crafts to vintage clothing, there is something for everyone in DC's bustling markets and boutique shops.

One of the most popular markets in DC is the Eastern Market, which is located in the Capitol Hill neighborhood. This historic indoor/outdoor market features dozens of local vendors selling everything from fresh produce and seafood to handmade crafts and gifts. Visitors can also enjoy live music and street performers while browsing the market's many stalls.

Another popular market in DC is the Union Market, which is located in the Northeast neighborhood. This indoor market features a variety of vendors selling everything from gourmet food and coffee to handmade crafts and gifts. Visitors can also enjoy the market's many restaurants and bars, which offer a range of delicious local cuisine.

For those looking for unique and eclectic boutiques, the U Street Corridor and Adams Morgan neighborhoods are both known for their independent shops and boutiques. In the U Street Corridor, visitors can explore stores like Meeps, which specializes in vintage clothing and accessories, or browse the handmade pottery and jewelry at Little Shop of Clay.

In the Adams Morgan neighborhood, visitors can find boutiques like Idle Time Books, which offers a wide selection of rare and used books, or shop for unique gifts and home decor at stores like Salt & Sundry.

Georgetown is another popular neighborhood for boutique shopping in DC. Visitors can explore high-end designer stores like Tory Burch and Ralph Lauren, or browse handmade jewelry and unique gifts at boutiques like the Tiny Jewel Box and the Phoenix.

Finally, DC is also home to a variety of specialty shops that offer unique products and experiences to visitors. The Smithsonian Museum stores offer a range of educational and scientific souvenirs, while the District Wharf neighborhood features a variety of boutique shops and outdoor markets.

Chapter6: Practical Information

Safety tips and common scams to avoid

Washington, D.C. is generally a safe city for tourists, but like any major city, it's important to take precautions to ensure your safety. Here are some safety tips and common scams to avoid when visiting Washington, D.C.:

1. Be aware of your surroundings: When walking around the city, be aware of your surroundings and stay alert to any potential dangers. Avoid going alone late at night and stick to well-lit locations.

2. Keep your valuables secure: Keep your valuables, such as your phone, wallet, and camera, secure and out of sight when in public. Avoid carrying large amounts of

cash and only bring what you need for the day.

3. Use reputable transportation: Use only reputable taxis, ride-sharing services, and public transportation. If you're taking a taxi, make sure it has a valid license and always agree on a price before getting in.

4. Avoid deserted areas: Avoid deserted areas of the city, particularly at night. Stick to well-traveled and well-lit areas, especially when walking to and from your accommodations.

5. Watch out for pickpockets: Pickpocketing is a common problem in tourist areas. Keep your belongings close to you, and avoid leaving your bags or purses unattended.

6. Be cautious of strangers: Be cautious of strangers who approach you on the street, particularly if they try to sell you

something or ask for money. Never give out personal information, and avoid engaging with anyone who makes you feel uncomfortable.

7. Avoid ticket scams: There are many ticket scams in the city, particularly around popular tourist attractions. Be wary of anyone offering discounted or free tickets, and always purchase tickets from reputable sources.

8. Be wary of ATM skimming: ATM skimming is becoming more common in the city. While utilizing ATMs, use caution and always use machines in well-lit, public locations. Before operating the machine, inspect it for indications of manipulation.

9. Be cautious of street performers: While many street performers in the city are legitimate, some may try to scam tourists. Be cautious of anyone who demands

money or tries to intimidate you into giving them money.

10. Be cautious of charity scams: Charity scams are another common problem in the city. Be cautious of anyone who approaches you asking for donations, and always verifies the legitimacy of the charity before donating.

By taking these precautions and being aware of the common scams in the city, you can have a safe and enjoyable trip to Washington, D.C.

Money and budgeting in Washington DC

As a first-time traveler to Washington DC, it is important to have a basic understanding of the local currency and how to budget for your trip. This guide will provide you with useful information to help you plan and manage your finances during your stay in the city.

Currency: The US dollar is the official currency of the United States (USD). One US dollar is split into 100 cents, including coins in denominations of one cent (penny), five cents (nickel), ten cents (dime), twenty-five cents (quarter), and fifty cents (half-dollar). Banknotes are available in $1, $2, $5, $10, $20, $50, and $100 denominations.

Exchanging Currency: There are several options for exchanging currency in Washington DC. Most banks and currency exchange bureaus offer competitive rates for exchanging currency, and many hotels also offer this service to their guests. It is important to compare rates and fees to ensure that you are getting the best deal.

Credit Cards: Credit cards are widely accepted in Washington DC, and most establishments, including hotels, restaurants, and shops, accept major credit cards such as Visa, Mastercard, American Express, and Discover. However, it is always a good idea to carry some cash as a backup, especially when visiting smaller establishments that may not accept credit cards.

ATMs: ATMs are widely available in Washington DC, and most accept international cards. However, it is important to check with your bank to ensure that your card will work in the United States and to inquire about any fees that may be incurred for using foreign ATMs.

Budgeting: Washington DC is a relatively expensive city, with prices for food, accommodation, and activities generally higher than in other parts of the United States. However, there are still ways to save money while exploring the city. Here are some tips for budgeting in Washington DC:

- Accommodation: Consider staying in budget-friendly accommodations such as hostels or budget hotels. Alternatively, look for deals and discounts on booking websites or consider staying in the suburbs and taking public transportation into the city.

- Transportation: Use public transportation such as the metro or bus system to save on transportation costs. Alternatively, consider walking or renting a bike to explore the city.

- Food: Look for budget-friendly dining options such as food trucks, street food, or local markets. Consider packing a picnic lunch to enjoy in one of the city's many parks.

- **Activities:** Many of Washington DC's top attractions, such as the Smithsonian museums and National Mall, are free to visit. Consider purchasing a city pass or discount card to save on admission to other attractions.

Overall, with some careful planning and budgeting, it is possible to enjoy a memorable trip to Washington DC without breaking the bank.

Tipping and etiquette in Washington DC

Tipping is an important part of the service industry in the United States, including Washington, D.C. Here are some tips and etiquette to keep in mind when tipping in the city:

1. Restaurant tipping: In restaurants, it is customary to tip 15-20% of the total bill, including tax. You may tip extra if the service was outstanding. Be sure to leave a cash tip or add it to the credit card slip.

2. Bar tipping: When drinking at a bar, it is customary to tip $1-2 per drink or 15-20% of the total bill. If you're running a tab, make sure to tip the bartender when closing out.

3. Taxi and rideshare tipping: When taking a taxi or rideshare service, it is customary to tip 15-20% of the total fare.

4. Hotel tipping: It is customary to tip hotel staff for their services. For example, you should tip the housekeeper $2-5 per day, the bellhop $2-5 per bag, and the concierge $5-10 for exceptional service.

5. Other service tipping: Tipping is also expected for other services such as

hairdressers, spa services, and tour guides. The customary tip for these services is 15-20%.

6. Etiquette: It is important to be polite when interacting with service staff. Always say "please" and "thank you," and be patient if the service is not up to your expectations. Avoid being confrontational or rude.

7. Cultural differences: It's important to note that in some cultures, tipping is not customary or expected. However, in the United States, it is a common practice and is seen as a way to show appreciation for good service.

8. Tipping guidelines: If you're unsure of how much to tip, a good rule of thumb is to tip 15-20% of the total bill for good service. However, if you're not satisfied with the service, you can tip less or not at all.

By following these tipping guidelines and practicing good etiquette, you can show your appreciation for good service and have a pleasant experience in the city.

Language and communication in Washington DC

Washington, D.C. is a diverse city, and English is the primary language spoken. However, due to the city's diverse population, you may encounter people speaking different languages, especially in tourist areas. Here are some tips for language and communication in Washington, D.C. for first-time travelers:

1. English is the primary language spoken in Washington, D.C. Most people you encounter will speak English, including service staff, taxi drivers, and hotel employees.

2. Spanish is the second most commonly spoken language in the city due to the large Hispanic population. You may encounter Spanish speakers in some restaurants, shops, and tourist areas.

3. In some tourist areas, you may also encounter people speaking other languages such as Mandarin, Arabic, and French. Many tourist destinations and hotels offer multi-lingual services.

4. If you don't speak English, it's a good idea to learn some basic phrases such as "hello," "goodbye," "please," and "thank you" in English. This will help you communicate with locals and navigate the city.

5. If you want assistance, do not be afraid to ask for it. Many individuals in the city are kind and eager to help guests. If you're having problems conversing, consider

utilizing smartphone translation applications or a phrasebook.

6. It is important to be nice and considerate while talking with natives. Avoid using slang or derogatory language and instead, use formal terms such as "Sir" or "Ma'am."

7. If you're visiting from another English-speaking country, be aware that there may be differences in vocabulary and pronunciation. For example, in the U.S., "trunk" refers to the storage compartment of a car, while in the UK, it's called the "boot."

8. In Washington, D.C., many cultural events and celebrations offer opportunities to learn about different languages and cultures. Attend a cultural event or festival to immerse yourself in the local culture

and learn more about different languages and traditions.

Learning basic English phrases and practicing good communication etiquette can help you navigate the city and have a more enjoyable experience.

Medical emergencies and health care

As a first-time traveler to Washington DC, it's important to know about the medical facilities and healthcare services in case of any medical emergency during your trip. Here is some information to help you prepare for any healthcare needs:

Medical Facilities: Washington DC has a range of medical facilities, including hospitals, clinics, and urgent care centers. Some of the major hospitals in the city are MedStar Georgetown University Hospital, George Washington University Hospital, and Howard University Hospital. These hospitals provide 24/7 emergency services, as well as primary and specialty care. There are also several walk-in clinics and urgent care centers throughout the city, such as the Urgent Care Center of Arlington and MedStar PromptCare.

Health Insurance: If you are traveling to Washington DC from another country, it is important to have health insurance that covers medical expenses. In the US, medical expenses can be very expensive, and having health insurance can help you avoid high medical bills in case of an emergency.

Pharmacies: There are several pharmacies throughout the city, including CVS, Walgreens, and Rite Aid. Most pharmacies are open 24/7 and provide prescription and over-the-counter medications.

Emergency Services: In case of a medical emergency, dial 911 to reach emergency services. The operators will connect you to the nearest emergency medical services and provide you with instructions on what to do until help arrives.

Vaccinations: Before traveling to Washington DC, it's important to check with your doctor to see if you need any vaccinations. Some common vaccinations that may be recommended include the flu vaccine, hepatitis A and B vaccines, and the measles, mumps, and rubella (MMR) vaccine. It's important to take necessary precautions and to have proper medical insurance and vaccination to stay healthy and safe during your trip.

Wifi and internet access

As a first-time traveler to Washington, D.C., you'll likely want to stay connected while you're exploring the city.

1. Free Wi-Fi: Many hotels, restaurants, cafes, and other public spaces in Washington, D.C. offer free Wi-Fi. In particular, many of the city's public libraries offer free Wi-Fi access, and you don't need a library card to use it.

2. Paid Wi-Fi: Some hotels and other establishments may charge for Wi-Fi access. Be sure to check with your hotel or other lodging options to see if Wi-Fi is included or if there's an additional fee.

3. Mobile Data: If you're visiting from another country, it's important to check with your mobile provider to see if your phone will work in the United States. If it

does, you can purchase a local SIM card or a prepaid data plan to access the internet while you're in Washington, D.C. Most major carriers have coverage in the city, including AT&T, T-Mobile, and Verizon.

4. Public Wi-Fi Hotspots: Washington, D.C. offers free Wi-Fi in some public spaces, including in certain parks and metro stations. You can also find public Wi-Fi hotspots throughout the city, including at airports, cafes, and restaurants. However, it's important to use caution when connecting to public Wi-Fi networks, as they may not be secure.

5. Internet Cafes: If you need a dedicated workspace or reliable internet access, there are internet cafes throughout the city. Many of these cafes offer hourly rates and

have printing and scanning services available.

6. Wi-Fi Hotspot Apps: There are several apps available that can help you locate Wi-Fi hotspots in the city, including WiFi Map and OpenSignal. These apps can be useful for finding free Wi-Fi hotspots in your immediate area.

Be sure to take precautions when connecting to public Wi-Fi networks to protect your personal information.

Sim card and phone plans

As a first-time traveler to Washington DC, you may be wondering about the best options for a local phone plan and SIM card. Here's what you need to know:

1. Mobile carriers: There are four major mobile carriers in the United States:

AT&T, Verizon, T-Mobile, and Sprint. Each of these carriers offers prepaid and postpaid plans that may suit your needs. You can purchase a SIM card and phone plan from any of these carriers at their retail locations or online.

2. Types of plans: Prepaid plans allow you to pay in advance for a certain amount of data, minutes, and text messages. Postpaid plans are monthly plans where you pay for usage after it has occurred. They usually require a credit check and a contract. Prepaid plans are generally more affordable and flexible for tourists.

3. Where to buy: You can purchase a SIM card and phone plan at carrier retail locations, electronics stores, and online. The carrier websites often have the best deals and promotions. Make sure you have

an unlocked GSM phone that is compatible with the carrier's networks.

4. Coverage: The mobile carriers have varying coverage across the city. Verizon has the most comprehensive coverage, followed by AT&T, T-Mobile, and Sprint. Check the carriers' coverage maps before choosing a plan.

5. Costs: The cost of a SIM card and phone plan depends on the amount of data, minutes, and text messages you require. Prepaid plans start at around $30 for a month of unlimited talk and text with a few gigabytes of data. Postpaid plans can be more expensive, starting at around $60 per month.

6. Alternative options: If you do not wish to purchase a SIM card and phone plan, you can consider renting a mobile hotspot

device or using public Wi-Fi. Many cafes, restaurants, and tourist attractions offer free Wi-Fi, but be sure to use a virtual private network (VPN) to protect your privacy and security.

7. Emergency calls: In case of an emergency, you can dial 911 from any phone, even if it is not connected to a carrier network.

Emergency Contacts

As a first-time traveler to Washington DC, it's essential to know the emergency contacts to ensure your safety and well-being. Here are some emergency contacts to keep in mind:

1. 911: In the United States, this is the universal emergency number. When you dial 911, you will be connected to the closest emergency services, such as police, fire, or ambulance.

2. **National Poison Control Center:** If you or someone you know has been exposed to a harmful substance, contact the National Poison Control Center at 1-800-222-1222.

3. **Hospitals and Urgent Care Centers:** There are several hospitals and urgent care centers in Washington DC that you can contact in case of a medical emergency. Some of the notable ones include MedStar Georgetown University Hospital, George Washington University Hospital, and Sibley Memorial Hospital.

4. **American Red Cross:** The American Red Cross provides emergency assistance, disaster relief, and education services. You can contact them at 1-800-733-2767.

5. **Embassy of your home country:** If you are a foreign national, you can contact the embassy or consulate of your home

country for assistance in case of an emergency.

6. Metropolitan Police Department: If you need to report a non-emergency crime or need assistance from the police, you can contact the Metropolitan Police Department at (202) 727-9099.

7. Fire and Emergency Medical Services: For non-emergency fire or medical assistance, you can contact the Fire and Emergency Medical Services department at (202) 673-3331.

It's always a good idea to have these emergency contacts programmed into your phone or written down somewhere accessible in case of an emergency.

Useful apps and resources for visitors to WashingtonDC

As a first-time visitor to Washington, DC, there are numerous handy applications and tools that may make your experience more pleasurable and stress-free. Here are a few of the best applications and resources to consider:

Washington, DC Official Visitors Guide: This app includes thorough information on the city's best attractions, hotels, restaurants, and events. You may get it for free from the App Store or Google Play.

DC Metro and Bus: This app assists you in navigating the city's public transit system, including the metro and bus services. It gives real-time arrival and departure times, as well as comprehensive maps and itineraries. You may get it for free from the App Store or Google Play.

Capital Bike Share: Using this app, you may borrow a bike from any of the city's 500+ bike stations. You can find available bikes, monitor your ride, and examine your journey history. You may get it for free from the App Store or Google Play.

ParkMobile: This software enables you to use your smartphone to pay for parking meters and garages across the city. You may also see available parking places and book one ahead of time. You may get it for free from the App Store or Google Play.

Yelp: This app gives user-generated reviews and ratings of local businesses such as restaurants, pubs, and stores. It can help you locate the greatest locations to dine, drink, and shop in the city. You may get it for free from the App Store or Google Play.

Smithsonian Mobile: This app gives information on all of the city's Smithsonian museums and galleries, including show schedules, maps, and insider tips. You may get it for free from the App Store or Google Play.

OpenTable: This app enables you to book reservations at popular restaurants in the city, including Michelin-starred businesses. You may also explore menus and read reviews from other diners. You may get it for free from the App Store or Google Play.

Uber and Lyft: These applications enable you to order transport from a private driver and pay using your smartphone. They are popular alternatives to taxis and public transit. You may get them for free from the App Store or Google Play.

Google Maps: This software includes precise maps, instructions, and real-time traffic information. It can assist you to traverse the city on foot, by automobile, or by public transit. You may get it for free from the App Store or Google Play.

DCist: This website and app give up-to-date news and information about events, gastronomy, and culture in the city. You may use it to remain informed and organize your schedule. You may access it for free on their website or by downloading the app from the iTunes Store or Google Play.

These are just a handful of the numerous helpful applications and tools accessible to tourists in Washington, DC. By installing and utilizing these applications, you can make the most of your vacation and have a great time in the nation's capital.

Final thoughts and Conclusion

As a first-time traveler to Washington DC, you are in for a treat. The nation's capital is a city of rich history, culture, and beautiful attractions. From the impressive monuments and memorials to the world-class museums, Washington DC has something for everyone.

One thing to keep in mind is that Washington DC is a busy city with plenty of activities to do and places to visit. It is essential to plan your trip ahead of time to maximize your time and make the most out of your stay.

When it comes to public transportation, Washington DC boasts a well-developed system that includes buses, trains, and metro lines. It is a quick and inexpensive method to go about the city. If you want to hire a vehicle, there are various car rental firms in the city. However, it's worth considering that traffic can be heavy during peak hours, so plan accordingly.

There are several accommodation options to choose from in Washington DC, ranging from budget-friendly hostels to luxurious hotels. It is crucial to research and book accommodation ahead of time to ensure availability and get the best deals.

Washington DC is also a foodie's paradise, with plenty of local cuisine and specialties to try out. From traditional Maryland crab cakes to Ethiopian injera bread, you'll find an array of food trucks and street food vendors throughout the city.

While in the city, be sure to visit the top attractions, including the National Mall and

Memorial Parks, the Smithsonian Museums, the White House and Capitol Hill, and various monuments and memorials.

If you have time, explore the surrounding areas by taking day trips and excursions to Alexandria, Annapolis, Baltimore, Gettysburg, or Shenandoah National Park.

In case of emergencies, there are several medical facilities in the city, and it is essential to have a travel insurance plan to cover any medical expenses.

Overall, Washington DC is an excellent destination for first-time travelers. It offers an array of attractions, delicious food, and vibrant culture. With proper planning and research, you're sure to have a fantastic trip to the nation's capital.

Printed in Great Britain
by Amazon